Poetical

Musings

on Pianos, Music & Life

Volume I

♫♪♫

Ann Grogan

ISBN 978-1-970-10986-3
eISBN 978-1-970-10987-0

Fonts selected for this book are: titles in Chopin Script and text in Linux Libertine Display.

The image on front cover was taken during the rebuilding process of *Rhapsody-Arabesque* (*The Duchess of Music and Bliss*), a 1928 Steinway Model M and shows the soundboard after the original strings had been removed.

Published September 2023

From Our Readers

"I found your book enjoyable, funny, and sad. I had stopped reading books for enjoyment, and now mainly research practical topics on the computer, tablet, or phone. Your book brought me back to slowing down and reading for enjoyment."

> – Raven Crone, Wiccan, fabric artist, nomad, and amateur guitarist

"I teach guitar to youths who are delightfully inquisitive and open-minded. In my current cycle of teaching, we focus on learning about the process of manifestation and how to better connect their musical expression with their thoughts, beliefs, and values. After reading your poetry, I decided at the end of classes to select and read a poem that might offer my students insight into their personal musical journeys and inspire them to continue."

> – Tung Vu, classical guitarist, music producer, and guitar teacher

"Ann Grogan's *Poetical Musings* is bursting with whimsy, heart, and passion. She draws inspiration from neuroscience, the lives of composers, the ups and downs of her private artistic journey, tender childhood memories, and even a friend's playful and wise cat. Some poems, like "Wasting Time," I imagine set to a hip hop beat. Other poems, such as "In Flight," lilt with a romanticism heightened by rhyming couplets–reminiscent of the sensibilities of so may romantic era composers. Open the book at random and find delight! Ann's book is a testament to the power of saying yes to the call of creativity."

> – Elyse Shafarman, MA
> Certified Alexander Technique
> teacher (www.bodyproject.us)

"Ann's words are those of love of music to be sure, but also love of life, abundance, family, and humanity. Often whimsical, her poems do not belie her depth of emotion and passion for music and all art; she bares her soul frankly with both seriousness and lightheartedness. She understands all that is music: its essence, poignancy, and soul-stirring centrality to life. She imparts that profound connection to the reader with poetry that is fresh and perceptive. Her poems will inspire you to learn more, seek out more, and play more music!"

– Janine Borchgrevink,
piano teacher, artist
and architect

"Ann's clever word play lifts the soul taking you on a journey through music filled with excitement and laughter."

– Lisa Johnson, CMT, Reiki Master,
and Chi Nei Tsang practitioner

Dedication

To anyone who has a song in their heart to sing.

Acknowledgments

I'm especially thankful to my always patient life partner Ron Choy, to my careful volunteer editors Sheri Jurnecka and Joe Torres, OD, to technical music advisors Dr. Maureen Buja, Dr. Susan McClary, and Bruce Nalezny. (However, any remaining errors are my responsibility)

Introduction

As for poetry, I have no clue where that comes from, other than the deep well of a life-long creative urge to self-express and from time to time, share a personal story. I know that poetry is linked with my life's trials and triumphs. Lately I realized that it is linked with my deep love of music and the piano.

I began to write poetry about music after I awakened from a very long slumber of my creative self. Drowsiness came on almost imperceptibly over years, about 63 or so. Finally, I fell fast asleep as if I had taken a bite of the poison apple. My childhood enjoyment of the piano had deserted me. I forgot how during occasional times in the past that music had been a keen source of bliss, or provided therapeutic relief from the stress of daily life.

That I could in my senor years start writing about and making music on my old 1953 Baldwin Acrosonic spinet piano, and eventually on a gorgeous little rebuilt 1928 Steinway Model M *(The Duchess)*, was not evident to me until the spring of 2020.

One day while sitting at my computer shortly after we were locked down at the start of the pandemic in March 2020, I looked at my spinet to the right and the urge to play came to me again. This time it was full-blown and permanent.

In the fall of 2021 poetical musings followed with a vengeance. Almost every day I began pouring out what at my worst I call fine examples of doggerel or limericks. At my best I see a glimmer of both rhyme and truth in what I write. I've shared little of that, usually with only a few people who are members of my new Music Tribe. They received it well and continue to encourage me, so I persist and have shared it with you in this volume as well as in a second volume of poetry andmy grand piano search story which is in preparation.

Writing poetry provides solace and inspiration for me to keep on learning how to play the piano and pursue the bliss of music. Enjoy!

– Ann Grogan ♫♪♫

Fig. 1 *Rhapsody-Arabesque* (*The Duchess of Music and Bliss*) in her new home.

Table of Contents

On Poetry

♫♪♫

"It was at that age, that poetry came in search of me."

— Pablo Neruda, Chilean poet,
diplomat, and politician

Fig. 2   Ann plays *The Duchess* for the first time on
October 16, 2021.

shades of emily and ogden

i think that i shall never vu
a poem as lovely as a pianu
full of grace
in cabinet face
with sounds from bass to sopranu

True Bliss

I think in rhymes
Most of the time.
I cannot lie,
It mystifies
And does defy all reason.

Must be the season to dream aloud,
Speak silent, and rush so slow,
But as I go the shadows fall,
The sunset glows
And I recall there's only this:
True bliss comes short
As seconds burst
While I thirst
For so much more.

So what's in store?
I cannot say
But I can live and love
Another day!

Poet Laureate?

I may have to vie for Poet Laureate
Because my mind just won't quit it.
"What?" you say; "tell me, do pray."
That's easy: the obsession to rhyme
And continue in meteoric rise
With tempo fast and furious,
My tendencies so curious,
From where I've no clue.
I wonder, do you?
No matter the cause
I'd love to dispose
Of it all and be free
To finally see
An end in sight
And pure delight
To finally leave
This curse I rehearse
Each day down to moments
When poetic thoughts foment
In rhymes not particular,
Some solid, some vesicular,
All whirling around.
The images abound
From love to fright,
From fear to delight.
May this affliction depart
And never restart!
Or maybe stay here
As I reduce fear
And learn to appreciate
My current state?

Dreaming In Poetry

I dream in rhyme
And wake with poems
Swimming in my head.

I wonder what it means,
From where they come,
If good, or should I dread?

Consuming me,
Poems dance and shift.
Should I wake up instead?

And why now
And not before?
Was it something that I read?

Or always part
Of me and so
With them I should wed?

Who cares I say,
If they intrude
And on my sleep do tread?

I'll stay right here
And will pursue
Those dreams: full speed ahead!

About Writing Poetry

They say she died buried alive
In poems a pure mile deep,
But then some doggerel
Began to hound her
And put them all fast asleep!

Why Words Flow

So easily the poems come
And oft-times pure doggerel
About the topics of the mind
And all things psychological
Or silly or social or erudite.
But what's most to me of fascination,
What holds me so enthralled,
Is human behavior in its ramifications,
And what focuses me and my fertile brain,
Gathering neurons to fire in conjunct,
Are thoughts of you, then poems do flow
In rapturous words, sometimes succinct.

Sometimes

Sometimes my poetic muse
Joins me with a thought,
A whispered word, a deed observed,
Or information sought,
Or news story heard.
My muse, she then comes forth,
Grabs me by imagination
And words do flow
And outward go
To express what I feel
Or think or know.

On How to Write Poetry

You won't know unless you try,
You won't do it 'til you care,
You'll feel no bliss 'til you love,
You won't enjoy it 'til you share.

Stop a moment, sit right there,
Let your muse say hello,
Be still, be aware
As you call her from below.

A poem often dwells
In shadows so soft
Or in dreams that will always
Carry you aloft,

The one that you know
So clearly, so well,
Or the other that in mist
Sometimes does dwell.

The words will come
If you but allow
The truth I espouse
And my advice, follow.

Take your pencil up
And do what I say,
But it helps a good bit
To laugh, and then pray!

To Thank You

It's purely a labor of love this is,
My modest poetry booklet.
You* urged me to gather my poems up
And publish without regret.

So not knowing where your idea could lead
But liking the goal I could see,
I plunged right in to dot my "i's"
And take care to cross my "t's."

It wasn't until the third proof came
That themes began to show
And questions about why I first began
Inside my head did flow.

Two reasons soon came to me,
The first was very clear:
To remind myself of my life's paths
And the values I hold dear.

But crept in, too, the idea that
To thank you I did try,
For receiving the joy I needed to express
About my soul and life.

---

*Bruce Nalezny, pianist, composer, Director/
Founder of The Piano Gallery and piano broker who
located *The Duchess* and first suggested that
I publish my poems (bruce@finepiano.com).

On Music & Musicology

♫♪♫

"Come, follow me into the realm of music...Here there is no end to the astonishments, and yet from the beginning we feel it is homelike..."

— Ferruccio Busoni
(in a letter to his wife);
Italian composer, pianist,
conductor, editor, writer,
and piano teacher

Fig. 3 The day Ann finds her *Duchess*, October 16, 2021; faded glory from 1928, a Steinway Model M.

The Mockingbird

You cannot argue with music as with words.
A melody is soul expressed and heart contoured
In line and note. But rest assured
'Tis beyond that, that we are stirred
To express ourselves as we are spurred
To do. Music rules without words.
To argue contra would be absurd;
A song is more than just one word–
Just listen to the mockingbird!

Reborn

I am a snake who slipped her skin,
Who slithers now toward birth within.
Left behind in dirt and slime
Remains the shell. Now life divine
Beckons me. No waste of time
Can ever be again. No hate, just rhyme
Can carry me to more of me and unity
Of passions all. Music, art, and dance, those three
Beyond reproach, or cause, or quest–
None of them prevail as best.
The same, all three, the mind and body and spirit be
Just one, even as you and I can see
If we but stand and look
Beyond the page of score or book:
Divinity in unity–all things and beings
One and same. Through gift of sight, eternal spring.

A Thing Apart

To make music is a thing apart,
Akin to thoughts of craft v. art.
It's more than talent that's required
To score or play a thing inspired.
Some say that rhythm's what's at base,
While others argue tunes the place
That births true art, but then, who cares?
To obsess on that would surely err.

For those who play don't just perform,
Nor do they seek to us inform,
But rather deeper go inside
To where their muse, she does reside,
And coax her out for some to hear
Or all delight who are lucky, near.

Maestra, maestro, both endowed
With desire that burns beyond what's allowed
To self-express, though *no one's* near,
A melody from soul so clear.
They can't *not* play or sit aside
Quietly, just along for a ride,
But must expose from inside out
Their soul, compelling song to shout
Or whisper soft as desire dictates
And art our world does permeate.

Friends

There is no need to want me
For other than your friend,
But briefest note or imagined sigh
And to your will I bend.
Beware if you say you know me
In music or in art
Or say you share my taste in those,
Then I shall fall apart
And languish then in resignation,
Both hot and sweet by turns,
And strive to still the quake within
And quell the heart that churns.

What Reigns Supreme?

Not words or music are supreme.
To neither one should you cling
But welcome both with open arms–
Different lovers with different charms.
The two may never, ever unite
But both combine to cause delight.
Not value given by general consensus;
The worth comes from one's senses.
Music then, is not a toy
Though it gives the greatest joy,
Nor is it pure frivolity
Though it fills the soul with glee.
For logic in music inheres within
The playing of a song or what one sings
Or listens to. All count at last
Since none the other does surpass.

Speak Music to Me

Speak music to me and you'll get my attention;
Talk contour and rhythm and tempo and tone,
Timbre and pitch and melody, too,
And especially esoteric, the overtone.

Thrill me with romance–the musical kind,
Play classical piano and chills will ensue,
Join in my wonderment of sounds and you'll note
That clearly my heart will come along, too.

But more than the heart comes with musical joy
When tones reach inside and resonate wide
And connect me so easily with like-minded souls,
As waves unify the shore with the tide.

So wish you to know me? Then see if you see
Those parts of yourself reflected in me.
Speak art to me, then, and a friend you will be
From moment to *this* moment of eternity.

The Gift

The moment that we discover,
Be it melody or thought,
Something that connects with soul,
Familiar or newly taught,
Our spirits come awake from sleep,
Our feelings, so on fire!
They vibrate in the wonder of
Discovery and desire.

No matter how we learn or think,
Two things proceed them both:
Curiosity must inspire our mind
To open to the growth.
But blessed be those who care
And understand the pull
Of desire to share enacted; both
Receive the gift in full.

Wasting Time

Have you time for negativity,
Indulging in relativity,
Debating right or wrong?
It's all just one's opinion
(Sometimes overdone),
Like birds' differing song.
But truly blissful and unique
And worth what we might seek
Is what us all does join:
A love of life and nature blest,
Music, art, the bumble bee,
Fierce joy* and sweet repose,
A sunset, sunrise, even more—
Things we cannot keep or score,
Love and warmth...perhaps a rose?

———
*Inspired by Pilar's song and album of the same title;
https://www.youtube.com/ watch?v+PUIWr-Cb260

Nothing is Permanent*

The cult of precision came about in the 60s,
but today it's met with derision.
Since the 80s it seems that fluidity's back in style
for performance—the ubiquitous decision!

———

*Points made about the development of musical preferences
and styles in *The Rest is Noise, Listening to the Twentieth
Century* by Alex Ross.

The Keyboard

Bottom A to highest C?
These our life's range
Of choices be.
Within one keyboard
Of eighty-eight keys
Inhere all chances
And possibilities.

What will you choose?
What will befall?
What'll lead you on
Or progress forestall?

The choice is yours
From what you control;
Not much it seems,
Unless you be fooled
By thoughts of grandeur
And powers untold.

Lie back! Relax!
Let life unfold!

Interludes

Sweet interludes in morning come,
I know not when or why,
But goddess blessed me such that, then
My heart in joy does cry
And smile to think my friend does think
Along lines same as me
When across his mind does come
Our shared musicality.

The one suggests, perhaps provokes
The other to attend,
Discerning, then to share again
Our thoughts, so well they blend!
And souls do, too, as kindred spirits
Do greet the morning's light,
Our ears attuned, our waking hearts
Aflame in pure delight.

The moment's here—and then it's gone,
Our thoughts in soft repose
As on we get with daily tasks
Though they be otiose.
For meaning lies in what we've shared
No matter quick or long,
And hope resides, perhaps in both?
For another day—and song.

Musing*

May I be your amanuensis?
Carry your water or write your thesis?
Perhaps I can be your arborist,
Trim your trees, grind your wheat to grist?
Wipe your brow or turn the page
As you compose or as you rage,
Your amazing genius on full display
When on your piano you do play?
May I lie beneath your instrument,
Soak up your trills so heaven sent?
Or find the things that you may lose,
But most of all—just be your muse?

___
*Imagining George Sand's love for Chopin and how she
preferred to listen to him play.

16

The Basic Truth

There's no sound without motion
Or lovers without heart,
No smile without eyes,
No end without start,

No road without pebbles,
The same with a bridge,
No mountains without rocks
Or cliffs without edge,

No stars without blasts
Like the royal Big Bang,
No fire engine allowed
Without a loud clang,

No sight without photons
That our eyes can receive,
No coffee without beans
Or deep love without grief,

No music without genius
Or scores without notes,
No bliss without babes
On whom grandmoms can dote,

No apples without seeds
Or crops *sans* sunshine,
No chickens without eggs–
Or the opposite, we find?

No matter the causes
It's basically true:
Most wondrous of all,
There's no me without you.

Within

What attracts my mind, attracts my soul,
Then body follows suit;
It's first the one joined with the other,
And the third in hot pursuit.

Court me well, ideas first
In words, then roses next,
Plus a poem with rhyme or not,
And along come all the rest.

But music's better, the stuff of soul
In tempo, rhythm, and rhyme,
Show me song and then your heart
And next, I'll show you mine.

For all connect, the One and Same,
None standing side apart,
But be-all, end-all, bliss and joy
Begin within the heart.

Give Me A Round World

Levitin* says society has to train
Our children to be "civilized,"
To not stand and shout and dance about
Upon hearing songs so musical,
When movement inheres in rhythms magical–
To suppress that is completely tragical!
And yet "we" do, to maintain cohesion
And order and stuff so nonsensical.
Goddess save me from a world like that
Of suppression and affect so boringly flat!

————
*Daniel J. Levitin, *This is Your Brain on Music:
The Science of a Human Obsession.* Dr. Levitin is a neuroscientist,
musician, author, and James McGill Professor Emeritus of
Psychology, McGill University.

Settle?

There's no time in life to wait or settle
For what we want to do,
Or have or love or seek to find,
Or choose what we know is true.

For life is just an instant—here
Then gone beyond our grasp,
A sigh, a shout, a leap, a thought,
And sometimes just a gasp.

So fall you now a victim to
The judgment of another,
Or worry who is standing there,
Perhaps your dad or mother?

You, then, must choose your fate,
Recognize the gift or curse,
Accept or not what passes by
For better or for worse.

For no one else is there to choose
Or captain your own fate.
Beyond time now to steer your boat
To treasures that may await.

On Which Music is "Best"?

What is "natural" is not better
Or "natural" at all.
Music in the Western world
Is preference after all.

But "nature" calls us to acquit
What we believe is best.
'Tis only choice or habit set
But not from God is blest.

Some Days

Some days are like this,
Full of words–or music
That has no words.
Soft like feathers on a bird
Whose flight comes unbidden
Yet song, yes! Heard!
Inspired by who knows who
(She knows but cannot say),
Or what, or when?
She cannot write the largest part
Lodged deep within and quiet.
No use a pen.
So she retires, a quick retreat,
Sets pen aside in haste,
The answer clear.
When words desert the feeble mind
And feeling all that's left,
The piano's there!

Words vs. Music

"Words divide, tones unite,"
Upon that thought some would fight
And argue contra. They're one and same,
At least they play in the same game:
One a pitcher, one at bat,
One a mouse, one a cat,
Then they change as in cartoon,
One a hero, then a goon.
Why bother to divide the words?
That kind of fight would be absurd.
Step above to see the truth:
It's all one thing, forsooth!

Does Music Make Sense?

In my head is lingering
A notion I just read.
So silly this, it boggles the mind,
Yet of musical philosophers,
Some do find it true. You?

That music has no sense
Though rhythm it has and more,
But for Kant and Hegel
It holds nothingness,
No intellectualism in the score.

They claim music forces us
To listen. Really? How can that be
When so easily we flip the channel,
Click the button or swipe away
Any ear-trauma that we hear?

Perhaps if they were here today
They might think otherwise.
At least we can hope that they could cope
With rap and reggae and indie rock,
K-Pop, Benga, and Japanese folk.

On How Music Enthralls

Music, like sex,
Builds excitement
And perhaps will perplex
By not giving us
What we normally expect.
Syncopation raises tension
And I'm sure there are ample
Other clear examples.
My point here being
That music and a lover,
As we are now seeing,
Are one and the same,
Not two, but one game!

The Day

As morning sun or cautious grey
Paints the skies from bright to banal,
So rise my waking thoughts of you.
I muse, which feeling is veridical:

The one which grows from tiny seed
To firmest oak that will endure,
Or t'other that a season lasts,
And then moves on as does its lure?

The one which strikes a power chord
That trembles deep in harmony
Divine? Or the other, enfeebled so
It fades to something surely phony?

Perhaps a river which gently weaves
A pattern purely curvaceous,
Or t'other whose fullness winnows down
From wet to nothing more than dust?

The one whose rays shoot to the stars
Like fireworks create a gleaming blast?
Or brilliance belies the coming end
And smoke is all one sees at last?

But then perhaps, cathedral bells
In lofty halls will call us forth,
Or will profane subsume us both
And then we miss the glorious truth?

So what is truth or happiness?
Neither brooks common fear or caution,
But nothing more now can be said,
'Tis only to be seen and done.

Creativity

The urge to feel, "sensate disturbance,"
R. Witkin* says, is prime.
A theme is next, then we choose
The medium we refine
By practice and instruction. Thus,
We approximate our goal,
Like Indians circling wagons tight,
Come closer ever yet,
Each circle smaller and more bold
Before the blood is let.

The urge, society tamps down,
A heritage so puritanical,
Creativity conjoined with "out-of-control;"
To reason, so "antithetical?"
That thought and idea a gift, we see,
From our British inheritance.
Better said, a curse instead.
With benefit? No chance!

For feeling deeply is true art,
And expressing it the same.
To do less every day
Would surely be a shame.
And what is life but sensing it,
Next saying what we observe,
Then expressing how we feel–
That's surely how we learn.

---

*Robert W. Witkin, *The Intelligence of Feeling*
Dr. Witkin is Professor Emeritus of the University of
Exeter, United Kingdom, and an author who wrote
about topics in the sociology of the arts.

Musical Neurology

The neurons, they fire,
Then rockets explode,
The mind it goes
Into musical mode
As harmony it seeks,
A perpetual motion,
A rhythm to move by,
A thematic notion,
A nuance expressed,
Interpretation so fine,
Dynamics from loud
To softness divine.
With chills down her back,
And stars in her eyes,
Bliss envelops her in
A world of sighs.
All neurons alert,
Synapses so wide,
She floats on her cloud
Completely shut-eyed.
Be it our glorious body
Or the brain inside,
It's still from the soul
That pleasure derives.

Suspended Time

With you, my musical friend,*
Time has no beginning or end.
The hour set is much less
Important than the cause:
To merge together our musical souls,
Inspire the other, stretch our minds,
Call out our muses, gently hone
Our musical dreams and sweet desires
To please the senses and inspire the souls
Of those who listen in blest repose.

So much I seek in those quiet moments' cause,
Suspended in what's at hand
When we lend our pianos to the endeavor,
Or pass our time exploring the rhyme
Or reason of some musical theory.
So dreary that theory seems to me,
So often, too! Yet you encourage me
To persist though I resist and want to
Jump the gun, leapfrog over what must be done.

The sun's out tomorrow, a picnic's in store
As Mother Nature's glory shines.
We'll merge our thoughts, examine all,
And lunch at leisure in suspended time!

———
*One of the keenest pleasures derived from my newly
found love of music and the piano, is the periodic
lunches I share with Joe Torres, my neighbor pianist friend.
This poem and the one following, were inspired by him.

The Shy Sensualist

He's not a sensualist,
Or so he says,
My piano friend.

But he does show me
Right into his soul
Of sensual delight
In touch, in taste, in color, in sound,
In tone and contour,
And fabric, too.
His mood on clear display, it's true!

His ready smile makes me smile
When we come to share our song.
It causes delight in times
When we meet
And share our love so deep
Of music. So clear our connection,
And just as clear, his devotion
To the passions
And to the senses.

Not by thought bound,
Though intellect on full display
When we chat,
But for me it's far more than that.

Feelings flow as we go along
Sharing ideas of the day,
And then we play for each other
What we're working on.
Our song open for comment,
Generosity lent to every occasion.

A full blessing on that day sent,
A moment passed in pure bliss,
Our senses shared. A hug, a kiss,
We part, content.

To Love One Song

To love one song
Does not mean
I love the others less.
Each score is blessed
With blessed intention
By composers, all!

No one will fall
Into disrepute with me.
Not equal though they be.
Each one unique,
A gift the goddess gave
To man or woman,
Angels all who heard the call,
Took up their pen
To gift us all
With glories be:
Truth, passion, and despair,
Love, romance—it's all there
To thrill and chill our bones.

Sense comes from all the tones
Together. Then there's rhythm,
Contour and tempo,
Resonance and rubato,
Surely more,
Because the pianist who plays the score
Renders it a living thing
And total pleasure then does bring.

And as Proust said,
"Music is communication
Between souls."
Thus, to music we are called.

Musical Preferences

I like slow melodies,
Restful and wistful,
Serene and peaceful,
From sad to blissful.

Serene strikes my fancy
And then there's lyrical,
"Mellifluous," someone said,
Makes me wax poetical.

Schumann's my taste,
And then there's Chopin,
Effete as a raindrop,
Quintessential gentleman.

Just play me one note,
Arabesque* as it were,
And worries depart
As Debussy dissolves care.

John Field's close behind,
While Rachmaninoff's best,
Lohengrin's "Prelude"
Above all the rest?

Schubert delights
With his ineffable "Serenade,"
But a waltz by Lehár?
Merry Widow does lead.

And then there's "Naila,"
That transports to the heavens,
With repetitive arpeggios,
It leads to "Amen!"

---

*Arabesque No. 1 forevermore will be associated with
my appreciation of Joe Torres who accompanied
me many times in my search for *The Duchess,* and
commenced testing each piano by playing this piece.

Tell me a musical story,
Let's travel together,
Pull at my heartstrings,
Through all kinds of weather.

Touch me with care,
And the gentlest of sounds!
The piano's the thing
That lifts with no bounds.

Like tones of an angel
On dulcet harp strings,
The keys will produce
What melodies bring.

Music in the Movies.1

A composer's role, A. Copland* says,
What makes music serve the screen,
Are five items that move it forward,
To realize a producer's dream:
    - Create and convince about the place
     and time of all the action;
    - Enhance the thoughts of actors or
     give implication clear traction;
    - Fill the background with neutral sounds,
     smooth pauses between the clauses
    - Then tie together the errant ideas
     of various distinct parts
     that producer fails through lesser talent
     to unify from the start;
    - Or end it all in fits of glory
     and definitive exclamation.
Just name one movie with a silent end;
Without music, nothing's done!

---

*Aaron Copland, *What to Listen For in Music.*
The reader is warned to be prepared for insufferable arrogance
in charges that she has no musical taste if she concludes
differently from him.

Music in Movies. 2

Does a composer* save a movie?
A poor bit of acting, a bad line,
Or worse delivered? Save by bits
Or save it all when nothing seems divine?

And is it then a viewer's role
To ignore the music included there, Noting
only acting talent and
Fancy dress or costumes austere?

But no less important the music there,
The sonorous melodic touch
Behind the scenes and buoying up
A film that's loved so much.

———
*Inspired by Aaron Copland, *What to Listen for in Music.*

Music Inspires Excess

I have to laugh!
Music inspires insanity
Brought on by ecstasy
And also inspires excess.
Take Stewart's writing* on P. Olivera's life
And concept of "deep listening."
Stewart says it's not the words one says
Or shouts about or whispers,
But concerns itself with the doing of,
Then she writes 2000 words of airy-fairy prose
Extolling all the virtues of what her hero loves.
But follow her personal insight
Or heed her own advice?
Perhaps another time and place
She'll avoid her loquacious vice.

———
*Sharon Stewart says "Deep Listening...is primarily concerned
with the doing of listening, not saying what listening is or might
be for each individual; https//www.researchcatalog.net/view/
261881/261882/1811/5469

Pinker...or Darwin?

Pinker, Sperber, Barrow,* and more,
Claim that music is simply hedonic.
But from another perspective, some say,
That viewpoint is purely moronic.

Those three say music does not serve
A purpose or reason evolutionary,
That it cannot help predict the world
Or other things numerary.

But is biology the only way
We survive the challenges of this world?
And would our lifestyle be unchanged
If from our globe music were hurled?

Perhaps true that music does not impregnate–
But delightfully, my "first" at age twenty?
A handsome boy who wooed me with
His piano, in pursuit of his music degree!

So I think Levitin** wins the prize.
With Darwin he agrees on one evolutionary role:
To charm a lover one might want
And raise the passions in our soul.

Darwin said music's the peacock's tail–
Of course, a sexist implication
That only a male can woo the female.
Darwin needs an educational intervention!

———
*Steven Pinker, cognitive scientist, Harvard University;
Stanley Sperber, expert in choral music and conducting;
Lee G. Barrow, Professor of Music, Univ. of North GA.
**Daniel J. Levitin, *This is Your Brain on Music:
The Science of a Human Obsession.*

But endgaming results are our only drives?
To me, such a simplified view
As if the only important thing we need
Is the body, all else to eschew.

Besides, the issue of survival
Is truly a matter best called "red herring."
We're given far more than just a body;
To claim only that, untruth does ring.

Life is far more than sexual replication
And food for body is not the be-all.
We require music to nourish our soul
And, thus, a living death forestall.

Evolution, communication, words or thoughts,
Refinement of our motor skills,
All reasons to support the musical arts,
But those completely discount the thrills

That inhere when we let ourselves just feel
The passions, from lively to disconsolate.
We stretch our soul, our spirits soar,
Thus, our time on earth we elevate.

For more inheres in the life we're given,
A precious possibility from our universe
Of joy and bliss and transcendence;
A preview beyond we then rehearse.

It's not breath or cells required
To make it through this veil of tears,
But a desire to feel, express, and share
Our music to overcome our humanly fears.

What's Not to Like

"Dissonance," he says,
"Is one of many ways,
No less atonality,
Give opportunity
To experience far more
And how you may explore
And learn to appreciate
Movement and music's pace
Both internally,
And, as you'll see,
Even from without.
Of course, it may shout
Or quietly overcome
And leave you, oh, so glum,
Your silent expectations
Not there or delight begun.

"But trust you, and I pray
Continue, as some say,
To carefully attend.
Focus well, and then
Rewards will surely come;
A push beyond the norm,
Suspend all coming fear,
Open up your ear
No less your mind.
To habit do not bend
Or mindlessly descend
To banality.

"You will surely see
Rewards that before you lie.
Do not be so shy
Or rely on rank tradition.
Take yourself in hand;
This is your promised land!
Though I may sometimes preach,
Within your musical reach
Is clearly far, far more:
Bliss and joy in store!"

The Door

What is the crux of what I choose to like and play when,
Musically inclined, I open up my mind
And let my spirit loose?

Once open from inside,
A door exists for you to come inside.
And that requires far more than nonchalance
Or no response–even worse!
To me a curse, a repudiation,
And that I simply cannot take
Because I'll break, and that I cannot do.
So what do I choose?

It's not my job in life to judge music or another.
But it's my choice to share myself or music,
Be it with lover, friend, composer, all
(Mentors and performers included, too).
That pathway out includes a path within.
I open up my mind, my body, and
No less my soul to music as to a lover.
Those all the same; it's not a game to me.

It's reciprocation that I seek,
To see your door, open, too,
So I'm safe then to peek inside myself and coax her out
In whisper or in shout. Sometimes shy to speak out,
Sometimes bold, music pushes boundaries
And I become the women who live within:
The flirt, the angel, Miss Tinker Bell,
The nun, the dreamer, and all manner of what
Imagination brings.

A precious gift, those open doors,
But precious even more is what it takes
To just not break and stay inside:
Sometimes trust, and if I marshal it,
Courage.

I see us as the same in this non-game,
But different yet in life's experience.
We both shed tears, of course,
Yet each unique in
Different facets of a diamond dream.

What connects are glimpses
Of what shines within that is the same.
That is the music that I hear and choose.

Who Cares?

Who cares if composers create sounds
But no meaning inheres within,
Or only suggest what they felt?
Would either be a sin?

Who cares the meaning that they sense,
The feelings that they feel?
The point of music is to enjoy
The ride on *your* ferris wheel.

Though you're not a music expert
And no matter what you hear,
It's *yours* to say what meaning's there,
What truth to *you* is clear.

Remembering

Standing at my kitchen sink,
The warmth of water immersing hands,
Something reaches within to an unknown place
And a memory of Mom comes back unplanned.

Nearing now the ninth year
Since she opted to finally lie down,
Leaving me like all the rest
Of us who in life move on alone.

But in my pause from washing dishes,
A lovely thought came to mind:
The childhood gift my mother gave
As our creative natures intertwined.

It started with the joy of art,
As together we happily passed the time
Sitting on the floor to make
Collages with things we'd find,

Like feathers, sequins, crayons, and lace,
Finger paints, colored chalk, and glue.
We'd draw and paint some butterflies
Plus flowers and milk weed pods, too.

Then proudly, both, we'd hang them up
On my pink bedroom wall to cheer,
The reason, oh, so clear to me:
To see the enormous love we shared.

But best of all the gifts Mom gave?
My high school Baldwin spinet piano,
Far beyond my Mom's experience,
But somehow, somewhere deep she knew

To plant the seed and let it grow.
All these years the melody there,
Resting silent as life I lived,
Until at last I became aware:

Something called from deep within,
A need to self-express, a drive
To play again after so long,
A senior now, coming alive!

So many years now that you left me
To move on with life alone.
I wonder if when looking down
You see me thriving on my own,

Sitting at my sweet small spinet,
Striving to get better as I play,
Sometimes cursing, fingers overlapping
In the most frustrating, awkward way?

And so you smile, undoubtedly,
Because you taught me to persist!
Then you fold me in your angel wings
And strum your harp as we rise at last.

To Rocket

White and grey, I befriended him*
And he befriended me
While the boys were far, so far away
On wild, wild safari!
Too shy at first, he soon warmed up
And came around for soft pets,
Then treats, head rubs, and toy antics–
With belly rubs the best!
We rolled on floor together, then
He purred with total glee,
Approached, then ran away again,
Next rested alongside me
As soft and sweet *Sir B* I played,
On carpet deep he lolled,
In serious contemplation he,
A world apart, enthralled.

---

*Rocket is the kitty of my neighbor pianist friend
Joe. Often when Joe and his husband are away from
home traveling, Joe graciously permits me to visit
and play his gorgeous semi-concert grand piano,
Sir B, a special edition Beethoven Bösendorfer.
Rocket usually lies down by my side and dreams of
musical mousies as I play some of our favorite
romantic compositions.

To Cats

Were I a composer and especially endowed
With talents such that you would be wowed,
By writing notes of incredible import
That represent my subject of a cat-like sort,*
I'd choose something soft but also sinuous,
The paw held in air, the next step so tenuous,
The pounce that will come just as smile follows tears,
The bravery that follows the deepest of fears,
A back raised in hackles, the serious warning kind:
"Don't touch me, you fool, or I'll make you go blind!"
Or creeping around in the darkest of night
Just watching and waiting for the very next fight,
Or lolling in dreams curled up in a ball,
Or preening in sunlight, the quintessential femme fatale...
Were I that composer of the sweetest of dreams,
At piano I'd sit, lost in thought, as it seems,
And scribe a score so perfect in tone and in taste
That a cat would come through–if that were the case.

---

*Inspired by a delightful online article by Maureen Buja concerning
composers who wrote pieces about cats. Dr. Buja is an international
musicologist, writer, and editor; https://interlude.hk/cat-music/

To The Moon

There will come a day when I cannot play,
So shall I kill myself or waste away
Or even sit alone and mope?

Nope.
I'll smoke some dope,
Unfurl my hope and
Listen to what lives within.

Music never stops.
It seizes us and throws us in
Head first; that's how we learn to swim
Or ride bicycles.

When life cycles on and
Energy's almost gone,
I'll push a button and there they'll be!
Or melodies in memory flood in
From when I played

And then dismayed,
I'll hum them all in perfect tune
And voyage on to the moon!

On Composers, Compositions & Musicians

♫ ♪ ♫

There is only one real happiness in life
and that is the happiness of creating."

— Frederic Delius,
an English composer

Fig. 4 Ann in total bliss after playing her first semi-concert grand piano, with Joe at *Sir B,* his special edition Beethoven Bösendorfer, July 4, 2021.

The Mystery

Ah! The mystery of it,
The composer's soul,
Her talents and vision,
A story foretold.

His drive and his goal,
Then both enmeshed:
Technique and the dream,
With both he's blessed.

Where do they get it?
The mystery unfolds,
There's only one answer
That I now behold.

All melodies exist
Already composed,
Floating in air
But not yet exposed.

So one day she hears
A gossamer thread,
Reaches to the skies
Where her ear has led,

Grasps at the thread,
And gently tugs down,
This one then another
'Til many abound.

Then relying on grace
With undeniable talent,
She weaves a fine carpet,
Her time well spent.

But who is beneficiary,
The composer or us?
Who flies on the carpet?
The listener, of course!

We mount to the skies
On her inspired grace,
His vision completed,
The circle in place.

Three Things All Composers Face

I used to wonder how she did it,
Compose and not just play?
The idea? An easy source to see:
Creativity and the brain.
But two more things apply herein
And can stop her in her tracks;
The composer chooses but then must admit
What the instrument will lack,
No less the limits of the man
Or woman who performs
Combine to stump who would compose
To express love, defeat, or storm.

On Rachmaninoff's Piano Sonata No. 2

Who has lived
If not to hear this piece?
The Piano Sonata No. 2, I mean.
What other reason could there be
To explain life, than this?

Lest you go from this vale of tears
Before you hear it, take this time to listen.
Sit still; it will become you.
Become *you*.
Become you.

Electrified soul, with touch of just one key,
And all is said by Horowitz.
His tribute done, no crashing chords required.

Rachmaninoff sired this insane piece;
Horowitz birthed it,
Made it live.

Liszt

They said he thrilled ladies with his tempo,
They'd swoon and toss panties* at his legato,
He'd tickle the keys
Their harmony to please,
As they admired his prodigious rubato.

---

*To avoid confusion, Arthur Loesser reports that
ladies actually flung their jewels on the stage,
Men, Women, and Pianos: A Social History. Nonetheless,
Liszt was obviously quite the ladies' man.

On Nelson Freire's Death

May I have his* poise
To sooth my student's beating heart
From caring much too much
About the world without
Or other than what's there
And not the world within.

May I have his hands
To stroke a velvet tone
So my *Duchess* does not growl
But sings to me a lullaby
As clouds float by
And all around me rest.

May I have his smile,
A gentle grin from deep within.
A man who knows his place
At center of God's grace
And gives to all who thirst
And come after him.

———
*Nelson Freire (1944-2021), Brazilian
classical pianist, regarded as one of
the greatest pianists of his generation.

Pedantic

"Not a professional, even less a virtuoso,"*
So said C. Gounod about painter Ingres
Who loved to play on his sweet violin.
Yet Liszt said his play was "charming."
What's so alarming is Gounod's notion
So pedantic, not at all romantic
As Liszt would have it, and more;
Liszt dedicated the score
Of his transcriptions of
Beethoven's Fifth and Sixth Symphonies
To none other than his brother in music, Ingres.
So let's hear no more
Or criticism galore
Of those whose spirits soar
Though technique might not match
What you think they should,
Mr. Gounod!

---

*https://interlude.hk/jean-auguste-dominique-
ingres-1780-1867-fine-and-delicate-taste-is-the-
fruit-of-education-and-experience/

Saccharine?

"The saccharine teat of Romanticism"?*
As if there's sin in that!
To prefer music from the 1800s,
And all is lost in class?
What snobbery inheres within
A person who claims to have
The answers to what soars *my* soul,
But his soul does not salve.
So tell me not what I "should" like
And music I "should" curse.
'Tis best to leave it up to each;
To pontificate is worse!

---

*Inspired by comment, "Go back to the saccharine teat of
Romanticism if you can't digest the complexities of atonal"
posted by "joebassplayer after YouTube's *Transfigured
Night,* Op. 4 (an early composition by Arnold Schoenberg).

Midori

I think it's sad (and likely bad?)
To sit on high and think I can
Opine about music and what it means;
It needs no witty explanation.

I grab a thought and start to write,
Then hear Midori* the truth impart:
Music *is* truth, and then she says,
It's you as *whole*, not just a *part*.

And does she struggle, even yet?
Oh yes, she answers with a start.
The struggle inspires her to look further,
And lifelong learn about her art.

So shall I try, and try again
In puny efforts to express myself
And the meaning of the song within?
Music speaks for itself.

---

*Midori Goto is a Japanese-born American violinist.
She became a celebrated child prodigy, and today is
one of the world's preeminent violinists;
https://www.cbsnews.com/video/for-kennedy/
center-honoree-midori-playing-music-is=all=about-
learning-and-teaching/#X

What is Life?

Is life a dream as John Williams says,*
At the end of which we awaken?
Or is it less or more than that
When we reach the great "Amen?"

And does it go fast or slow?
"Six months of life at my age
Is a long, long time," he thoughtfully says
As he takes to the concert stage.

But never mind these ruminations
So common to us all,
The answer surely found elsewhere
And not in time at all.

Life's meaning resides so clearly
In truths that do not lie:
When hearing his "Theme" from *Jurassic Park*,
Said he was ready to die.

Even more so he did tell the truth,
And music did extol,
Because for him it's passion driven,
A necessity of body and soul.

A pastime and solace during pandemic,
For certain it was that,
But more for him "oxygen"
And the gratitude it begat.

_____

*Inspired by Javier C. Hernandez, "A Maestro
Looks Beyond the Movies," *New York Times*,
February 13, 2022. John Williams, 90, is a
prolific composer and pianist known principally
for his many popular movie theme compositions.

The Prelude to Act 1, Lohengrin*

The chill of crisp fall leaves
Floating with gentle breezes,
Prelude to winter.
Like *Lohengrin*'s angels
They descend on cloudy puffs of air
To give their gift.

Some oblivious to the miracle,
Some with eyes to see.
Shafts of golden light glow
Between falling pine leaves
As caramel oak leaves lie below
And glisten in the morning dew.

Too soon they come and then lie silent,
Gone, and we are left to grasp at meaning.
Memories of chills
That with each radiant leaf
Float up even as leaves fall
And sometimes echo
Silent as they rise again,
Like life.

Memories of times past
Felt in moments now:
What might have been,
A longing for a touch imagined,
A unity beyond grasp,
As inevitably the leaves at last
Retreat to heaven's ground,
And we rest.

---

*Discovered one dreamy fall morning while in a forest campground in California's Gold Country. The *Prelude to Act I* of Richard Wagner's opera is a musical depiction of the Holy Grail as it descends to the earth in the care of an Angelic host.

Arnold Schoenberg

Until today I did not know Schoenberg.
Why not?
My bad!
The lad, however inspired,
Does not touch me.*
I've tried.
Unique, his twelve-tone technique,
But then, I seek something else.

My ear hurts, but more so, my heart
To hear the torment
He must have felt inside his soul
To issue forth the sound that he molds.
No rhythm there nor tempo
Urging me to dance.
Askance, my ear listens to
What musically does not add up.

I could implore him and you
To forgive my narrow view,
My simple need to soar.
Dense in dreams of pure romance,
Perhaps I'll learn before life's burned,
That something's there, a gift perhaps,
And I'll abide what I hear.
But from what I hear,
That day's nowhere near.

---

*With one mesmerizing, romantic exception which
I adore: *Transfigured Night*, Op. 4.

Shock Upon Watching Salome

Jokanaan, oh! One of red viper tongue,
And Strauss the master of your fate!
What chills the soul beyond despair?
Salome pets the head of black, black locks
Then throws it to the birds of prey
Who lurking there, or dogs in lair,
Devour what has been done.

She, the child unborn, the slime desire come undone.
At last, the morsel repast or what is left,
The whitest white she sings of skin,
The blackest hair, the lust within unleashed.
To win her prize, this priceless diva*
Releases demons to unfold
And dances to show her liege, the king,
How easy will he bend to darkest dreams
That seized her soul.

Ewing, now having come upon despair
Waiting there to drown her from within,
Stripped bare to flesh upon the stage, now in her rage
And unjust reward,
Descends to kiss the mouth.
Her eyes o're-glazed with hellish glow,
Upon us all she does bestow
A deadly chill. We cannot look, we cannot leave,
Our soul with hers is interweaved
As all stare on the horror song
That takes us down with her.

So what is left when Strauss is done,
The deed begun by flesh made bare?
Who is to blame, what name the game?
The king? Her? Or love's deadly fang?
She sinks her teeth into our souls
No matter sun or fire.
Strauss takes us down with unremitting desire
That consumes us all, as *Salome* unfolds.

---
*Marie Ewing (1950-2022) an American lyric mezzo and full soprano opera singer known for compelling singing performances. Salome was one of her signature roles in Richard Strauss' opera of the same name. Her performance included a stunning naked dance sequence.

Offenses to The Romantic Notion

If *Salome* offends your senses,
Try staging by Hans Nuenfels,*
Especially *Die Zauberflote***
With the anti-Christ tales he tells:
The bald-headed fop, a fabulous drag queen,
A man holding a prick (or so it seems)?
Half naked the one, or tied up on a bed
And dressed all in white as if she will wed?
Was he eating a banana? She licking a needle?
Him pricking a priest who is offing a fellow–
Or was it a baptism? And what about him,
Knifing his wrist?
Oh the chaos of all! The horrible twist
Of imagination in riot,
A visual feast, an orgy in hell!

To explore him I followed the lead
Of the sad news memorial that I did read:
"Dead of Covid."
But of his boomer generation:
"One of the most inventive of directors."
How quaint! Almost hilarious! Just *one*?
When we are completely undone
By his visions on stage,
As dear Hans does rage and demand
Higher plaudits than that.
At least more than a pat on the back!
So please, just as he did, tell us the truth,
Hold nothing back. This man was far more
Than the hack you make him out to be.
More like a god was he.

_____
*Hans Neuenfels (1941-2022) was a German writer, poet,
film producer, librettist, theater and opera director and
manager. He was a leading exponent of German Regietheater.
**Mozart's opera, *The Magic Flute*.

Myung-whun Chung!

Myung-whun Chung!*

Discovered one blissful morn;
Grey day, grey skies
Freed focus and spirit to attend
And wend my way
Round Tchaikovsky's melodies:
The Sixth, "Pathétique" –
Without equal
I mean to say.

Is there more passion
Or abandoned control
We can find
Among conductors of the master Romanticists
That exist, than Chung?
Or for that matter,
A sweeter motif melody than that
Tchaikovsky sings?

I think not.
But then, I'll stop
Because there's no more to say
On this grey,
Most beautiful day!

———
*Myung-whun Chung is an exuberant, well-regarded
South Korean pianist and conductor who is committed to
musical and social causes in Asia; Principal Guest Conductor
Staatskapelle Dresden, and Honorary Music Director, Tokyo
Philharmonic Orchestra.

What a Composer Does

I see the composer,
At least of the sonata,
Develops the theme
In the middle, it seems,
As introduced at the first,
Be it blessed or cursed,
Then carries it forward
You understand.
So says Aaron Copland.*
And as I have learned,
The composer is then pressed
To find talents so blessed
And write developments pure
That really do soar.

What really must be
Are two things that I see:
The end section repeats
One or two former themes
Be they nightmares or dreams,
Then leads us to home
With a firm ending like stone,
So at last we are left
Feeling calm and not stressed.

---

*Aaron Copland, *What to Listen for in Music*. For the seminal 1991 feminist analysis of how tonality and the sonata form reflect prevailing 19th and 20th centuries' masculine-feminine binary tropes evidenced in Copland's description, see Professor Susan McClary's *Feminine Endings: Music, Gender and Sexuality*. McCrary is Fynette H. Kulas Professor of Music, Case Western Reserve University, Distinguished Professor Emerita, UCLA, and a MacArthur Fellow, 1995.

Taken Names

So why do they do it? Use taken names, I mean,
So unseemly when it leads us astray.
Take "Humoresque" to start.
I know the one by Dvořák,
And you will likely know it, too.
Hum along, and there's your song! But is it?

So why did Schumann steal that name?
(Or the other way around?)
For him, a game?
Is imitation the sincerest form
Of flattery, as a norm,
Or even in music, a proper form?

So will the real piece please stand up?
How can we know and then communicate
If the same word means different things,
No less a song title?
Ambiguity to eschew, vagueness even more,
In the same title for a different score!

Move on to concertos, some of pianos, some of cellos,
And then there's violins and next piccolos.
(Is there really? Yes there is:
Hear composer-pianist Amanda Harberg
Perform hers; so good there's no proper word
To describe it.)
Cantata this, cantata that...and etude after etude.
Can't they be more creative
In titling feelings they exude?

Composers think with sounds and notes
And then with tempos and keys,
But first come melodies which may echo
Someone else's, but they always find a way to show
A different vision, different meaning,
With a different persona beneath the thing.

So why not choose a title, give us a clue
To what they mean or what they saw?
It's hard enough to listen and not be misled
By titles reused, as I've said!

Listening

I'll diss no one who lifts a pen to write a score,
Though I may snore through some
When played for me. A million pardons I beg you
Who do compose those songs that pass me by.
Some will stick, some will thrill,
Chilblaines bring while I sit still
Or agitated be, if lifted to the skies
On Valkyrie wings of fire.

A lyre, a flute, sometimes a horn,
Oboe wistful or tinkling bell,
A cymbal brash and then drums crash–
And I'm left breathless!
Piano plays, the keys are lent; who plays?
Depends on how your thoughts are bent
Toward one of three: musician, music,
Or the instrument.

All composers merit our humble thanks,
Our love for courage that they found
To show their souls, no matter what befell,
Some poverty, some glory, as history tells.
But we give part meaning to their lives
And honor them, by listening.

Sante Parole *

Alone, but not alone.
Still, but not still.
Calm, but rising up,
Wafting on wings of the notes that angels sing.

So inspired were Reverberi and Giordano,
A heavenly match of two pure angels
Who reached through the clouds and stars
And happened upon the sound of this,*
Floating through the valleys of blue,
The first dusting of snow,
Forever light and lighter.

May they be blessed forever more,
And furthermore,
May I request that I be blessed
With this playing as I depart
This world, my spirit unfurled
And moving on, unfolding as behind me
Plays the darker day, and light moves me on...
And on.

*Italian for "holy words."
**"Notte Amalfitana" by Gian Piero Reverberi and
L. Giordana from the amazing 1980 album, *Rondo Veneziano*.
In 1979 Reverberi founded the *Rondo Veneziano*
chamber orchestra and he is their main composer,
arranger, and conductor. The group plays original
instruments, incorporating a modern rock-style rhythm
section comprising a synthesizer, bass guitar, and drums.

Home

(Those who compose may be excused;
We cannot love our babes less that those
Born and raised by others, so do not bother
To include here, those lucky souls
Who put bliss to score—and more.)

I wonder who has done it best of all
And answered the call of music?

I listen to this or that,
I try Mozart but he leaves me flat,
No less Beethoven and Bach, too,
Though I may rue saying that
When my next piano teacher happens on
This poem.

How can there be but one answer, one home
Along our way?
Though Prokofiev may thrill or salve my soul,*
And next Rachmaninoff, from "Vocalise" to "Daisies,"
Or playing duets with Kreisler
To explore love's loss** with notes, not words.

I've heard a lot by now, including Berg and Krenek,
Creative sorts with lots of meaning in their music,
Or perhaps, none. So be it.

"Music" all? Perhaps for some, or not for some.
No matter. All that matters is that
Hearing Chopin,*** I'm time and time again,
Home.

———
*Listen to his Symphony No. 7!
**"Leibesleid," composed for the violin by Fritz Kreisler then arranged for
piano, played by Rachmaninoff with Kreisler.
***There is but one perfect interpreter of Chopin for me,
and that is Chilean pianist, Claudio Arrau, whom I met on
records in high school through the perspicacity of my mother;
listen to his album, *Chopin: the 21 Nocturnes*, recorded in 1977-78.

Last Minute

"Need a last minute piece to play"
On your piano so sweet,
For this glorious Easter weekend?
A marketing piece
Found on one website
Where I usually find
The score I'm looking for.

But "last minute?" Seems so quaint,
So odd that anyone could
Find playing a piece would be
"Last minute?" Could there be soul in it
If such an ephemeral effort?
An impetus just caught on the wind,
Circulating there, waiting to be thought of
Then reached for.

Nothing is casual in music. All is deep,
Me, lost in thought, lost in hearing,
Lost in striving to express
The music I hear with which I'm blessed.

Though it came to me toward the end,
Music's not "last minute," but never ending.
Always there, waiting for me to hear,
To awake, to reconnect with all The Greats
Who play for me from past and present,
Their passions lent to spark mine,
Their minds bent to self-express
A heaven that they heard, notes they saw;
And so, they lead me on
In never-ending song.

The Labyrinth

I have been dropped, naked and afraid
Into The Labyrinth* of musical treasures.
The goddess saw fit, though I was not equipped
To do much else than just give in.
I could not swim; I had to stand, then walk,
A baby first, with such a thirst to drive me on!

I was scooped up, flailing in protest,
Not at my best, asleep as mainly one is
Before the Mystery unfolds
Of music soft, of music bold,
Portending pleasures exceeding what
We can imagine but never fully hear,
And dropped full stop midst curves so sinuous,
Continuously unfolding as I stumbled along
To follow her siren song.

I resent them all! Those who know, or mostly do!
They do not tell, but abandon me to blunder on,
And on and on....What will I miss now, in my hurry
To carry on, seize the day and find my way out...
Or in, as the case may be?

———
*Inspired by happening upon YouTube's video of the Paris
Symphony playing Prokofiev's Symphony No. 5, then discovering
Mendelssohn's "Contemplation" one day when sifting through
stacks of scores at a wonderful old, cluttered bookstore in Jackson,
CA. Will these serendipitous surprises never end (as I pray they
will not!)? Upon discovering the Fifth, I immediately exclaimed to
a musical friend: *"In THIS order: a hot shower, sex, and being inside
The Labyrinth!"*

Oh, That Aaron!

How is it that Beethoven
(At least in Copland's mind)*
Is "greater" as a creator
Than Ravel, as he does find?

Then says his opinion is
That sound varies with each composer.
Doesn't that confuse his point
And prove these two just differ?

But for some men, I guess
Life's seen as a grave contest:
One on top, one below
"Then pray! Forget the rest!"

So consider this, Mr. Aaron,
Swallow down this bitter pill:
It's not a contest with winner take all,
When to *any* music we thrill.

———
*Aaron Copland, *What to Listen for in Music*.

No Go

"Music is whatever musicians say it is."
So said John Cage
From his composer's gaze.

But I ask then, what role is left
For us hapless mere mortals
To have any part at all
In shaping the sounds or meanings of
What those of us who cannot compose,
Hear?

The element of chance causes me, at least,
To look askance at what Cage calls "music."
From his lofty solo post
He claims the sounds of room noises
That surround a silent piano
(Worse yet, a waiting maestro sitting there)
Are no less, no more, than "music."

Really? To him it may be so;
To me? A clear "no go."

———
*In John Cage's 1952 piano composition "4'33","
the performer is famously instructed to sit at the
instrument in silence, for four minutes and 33 seconds.
Admittedly, it is an interesting experiment in learning to
listen if you decide to watch this composition presented!

One Thing With Which To Agree

I found one thing with which to agree
In Copland's book,* don't you see,
In telling us "what to listen for,"
(I won't point out his grammar, so poor).
Without his typical arrogance,
At Stravinsky's view Aaron looks askance.
Said the former, music has no meaning
But's only an "object" and just "a thing."

Said Copland, "Wait a minute!"
We can't deny there's expression in it,
At least it has the right to be
Expressive. But what's the key
To what's expressed? Aye, there's the rub!
There's no one idea that we can snub.

Music expresses at different moments
Feelings that run from love to regrets.
So long as we have a general concept
Though with words we aren't always adept
Enough to easily describe the work,
There's no need, save to find a framework.

----
*Aaron Copland, *What to Listen for in Music.*

In Flight

1997 and Richter* leaves the world.
Where was I?
Awash then, in sleepless nights
On sofa in my back boutique,
Struggling, outside myself with worry,
Nightmarish garish dreams,
Always in a hurry,
Order this, selling that,
Collapsing boxes, shelving product,
Cleaning carpet, wasting time
That could be spent listening
To the angels sing in harmonies beyond
My wildest imaginings.

Where am I now? Home I think,
And waiting there all these years,
The tears I never cried from missing...
What? I do not know. I only know,
I've found it now, lost no more
But wrapped in shimmering, silver tissue wings,
Aloft, in flight, rising up, in love,
In music.

---

*Sviatoslav Teofilovich Richter (1915–1997) was a Russian
pianist who is frequently regarded as one of the greatest
pianists of all time and is reported to have had at least 3000
pieces in his repertoire.

Yudina: An Epic Poem

Scene 1

Poor Yudina,*
Such a crush had she once
That, when spurned, she turned on him
And offered up the gauntlet slap:
A duel! (A trap?)
He could but do her bid,
He faced no other choice
But submit. A woman scorned
Will not relent or avenging angels send
But go herself to take revenge
And let his blood like vampires do
When they wed and say "I do!"

One morning soft with grey aloft
She rose from slumber, self-possessed,
Dressed in crimson head to foot,
Took up her whip and called her brace.
With two black stallions in their place
Set off with Lila, her handmaid
And Second,the role she played
To the slaughter that was nigh.

Distressed? Yudina? Not at all.
Cold as the icy winds that howled
As rushed the steeds to the place of hell,
Guns strapped to her side as a Western Wench
Would wear, brandished, then at other times
Shown to friends and asked to hold them.
Who knows why? This time, decked out was she
With diamond crosses that she bore
And wore to concerts
That she gave, to raves about her intensity.

-----

*Maria Yudina (1899-1970), a Russian pianist and piano teacher.
According to Sviatoslav Richter in *Richter: Notebooks and
Conversations*, she was an excellent pianist, but overly intense in
her interpretations. Aside from (because of it?) the fact that she
was an eccentric character, audiences loved her. She was known to
carry a gun and ask friends to hold it, then warn them that it was
loaded! The story line about being spurned and the duel challenge
is true, but the results set forth in this poem are imaginary.

Impetuous to the max. Said Richter of her
Second Chopin Nocturne, "So heroic,
It turned piano into trumpet."
Was it scandalous? No word from Richter.
He didn't like her, that much was clear,
But did respect her virtuosity
If not the lady—
Such a curiosity for her time and place.

Scene 2
Disgraced (at least in her mind),
Yudina finds herself
In a bind and dedicated to vengeance
That she seeks to wreak.
He, defeated, goes to meet
His nemesis, Yudina. What a scene!

The stallions neighed and bucked and strained
As rainy pellets mangled manes
And blinded their full dash—to what?
Next scene, we'll see...stay tuned and learn
How love scorned did burn their hearts away.
But flay skin? Draw blood?
Depends on Yudina's mood
When she gets there!

Scene 3
He, waiting in despair,
His Second quivering more
Than Yudina's desired paramour.
Pacing now, his horse uneasy, too,
Tethered to a tree at edge of forest green,
Unseen the chilblains cascading down,
Niagara in full flow, thrashing sounds of
A heart in full retreat, or beating out of bounds.
He hears the crashing of her steeds
As any confidence proceeds to leave him,
Bereft of hope that he might prevail.
Regrets? You bet he has some *now*,
But not before when he scorned Yudina.

So nastily smug, he shrugged when she begged
To have a kiss. He missed the opportunity she gave
To live, had he but given in to lust
If not to love of her.
Spurned, she now returns with havoc on her mind.
Oh yes. I said that before...so what's in store?
Next scene we'll see...stay tuned and learn
What transpires when a spurned woman yearns.

Scene 4
So where were we?
A horse tied to a tree, two jellied males
Pale in face, beaded sweat foretold of fainting
Coming on, if Lila and Yudina did not get on
With their dastardly deed.

Take heed!
Steeds crashed through the brush
Then pulled up short with a mighty snort,
Their mistress clear she's one to fear
Lest she remove six shooters there,
Fire some warning shots, with a miss so near
To reddened cheeks.

So why is his Second so distraught,
A victim of love sought, but lost?
At what cost to two men there, the sin of one?
Both men undone!
(Let's keep them squirming a wee bit longer
While we ponder
What will dear Yudina choose to do?)

Scene 5
So here she is, the Woman of the Hour
Dressed in all her power
With murder on her mind.
Jumped off her chariot, drew her gun

(Just one of two),
Began to run at him with Lina close behind.
"Mistress–beware!" Lina yelled out
Because the lout, who staggered back
To fend off attack, had fainted flat!

(Was such a wimp deserving of her love–
Or lust, for that matter?)
How could she now shoot a fallen man
And take revenge? He beat her to the punch!
But even a maven such as she
Has principles galore.
She could not now proceed
By killing him with guns and metal.
What fine fettle and a mess she's in...
But close proximity to her victim
Should not be lost,
Without some cost to him.

Yudina stopped to ponder what to do.
She paced about and then she shouted
"Eureka! I've got it now!
Fair Lina, help me, please. Bring me the rope
And halter bit from the lips of one trusty steed."
"What could she need this for?" Lina thought.
"He's well caught for sure, but what's in store?"

I think I'll leave it at that
And to your vivid imagination
To see what doom the ladies fair
Have planned for the unfair lad
Who deigned to scorn a wench–
The wrong one, to boot.
What a hoot, I do declare!

The Little Gold Dress

Yuja Wang.* Need I say more?
A music-loving friend and I
Came to blows about her short dress–
Antipathy toward it, he refused to hide.

"Unsuitable for a pianist!" he insistently declared.
Beyond the edge he could tolerate,
Beyond concert decency as defined in his head,
And leading to loathing, perhaps even hate?

I pondered the fervor with which a gold dress,
Mini in style as Wang often wears,
Showing gorgeous slim legs and wearing stilettos,
Engendered his ire. As if anyone should care?

Such technical command! Such absolute precision!
(Though some might complain of perfect perfection?)
My curiosity piqued, I read with amusement
The raging debate over Wang's image presentation.

But times "are a-changin'" as Dylan shrewdly said,
And styles, they must flow and not be mechanical.
The dress kerfuffle clearly boils down in the end
To nothing more or less than a history puritanical.

Oh, yes. Don't forget that men like to tell us
How to dress and think and behave, no less.
So ladies, just ignore any misguided ire
And pursue your own version of Wang's little gold dress!

_____

*Yuja Wang is a 35-year old Chinese classical pianist. At the age of 22 she was an internationally-recognized concert pianist and today continues to tour internationally and receive critical praise for her stunning performances. Personally, I adore her concert fashion tastes!

On Music Theory, Piano Lessons & Practice

♫ ♪ ♫

Piano teacher to student: "You played that so well!
Better try it again to make sure it wasn't an accident."

> -- Suzanne W. Guy,
>   *Wit and Wisdom from the
>   Piano Bench*; pianist,
>   piano teacher, author, and
>   music editor

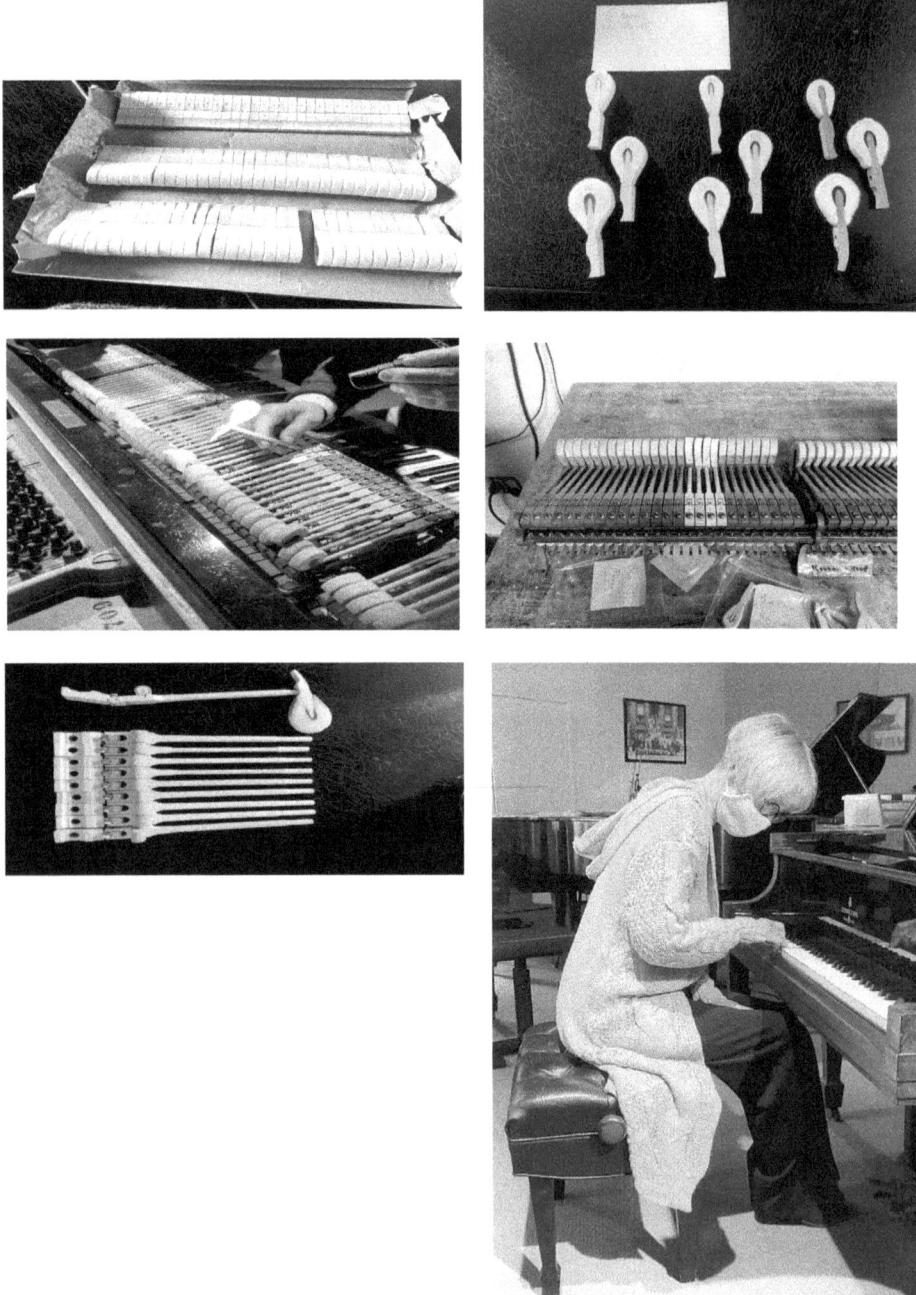

Fig. 5 Ann (along with three friends) tried out sample sets of five different piano hammers manufactured by two companies, and chose wurzen felt hammers from Ronson Piano Hammer Co. in upstate New York, December 14, 2021 (full hammer set pictured top l.).

Why Piano Theory Often Leaves Me "Flat"

I just became aware
Of when or why it is that
To study the "brain" of music–
Piano theory–leaves me flat.

As well, functions of the "action"
No less all component parts,
Are not intrinsically interesting
Unless they join to create art.

What is, is how a tone is made
And why a soundboard sings,
And how to express these better,
The melodies I hear and think.

So tell me something about how
The piano parts do work,
The why of touch and the overtones,
Then theory I'll not shirk.

The point for me is not
To be a great technician
And tune my grand piano
With perfection or precision,

But understand just how
Those join my mind with heart
And why they reach so deep within
To put theory in my art.

On Music Theory

Sometimes I reach a barricade
When light dissolves to dark.
I sink into a black hole
Of despair and do not care.
I feel so lost! I cannot cope,
I want to mope, I lose all hope.

I hate this feeling, so alone, so bereft
Of clue or glimmer of daylight.
Musical theory comes along fine
And then my brain-song
Completely disappears!

A seventh chord? The "iv" chord, too?
What the heck? How to find them?

I'm just so blind.

It takes a rope around my neck
Pulling me along
With donkey's feet planted there
In my despair.
No glimmer there,
My hope destroyed,
Distress instead
Inside my head.

Will I ever understand?
Meantime, I do just what I can,
Play my best, hang on tight
To music's delight,
Set aside my tears
And know someday it'll come along,
When theory connects to my inside song.

What Boggles Minds

All melodies are known,
Contained within the infinite,
Also the piano's keys
And notes you sing
Or do not sing–
Not imagining
How random are the scales
You know so well,
Chosen by another,
Not you. How true! You see?

In the infinite relationship
Mathematics of the tones we play
Are works of Bach,
Beethoven, too,
And likely even Schu(mann)!

But never mind what boggles minds
Of those of us who struggle
With shards of math
Or the infinite path
Of irrational numbers.
If such parts of you do slumber,
Close your eyes, just listen well
And soon you'll tell
My truth is true.

Composers seek the embers,
Remember all the notes they see
And bring their melodies from memory–
Always there.

Pick a Song

Pick a song, he said,
A melody that thrills,
A style that suits your fancy
And down your back brings chills.

Then tell me if you will,
But make it have both these:
Augmented and diminished chords
And answer, if you please.

She opened up Snell and Johnson,*
Two respected theory books,
To figure out his puzzle
But her mind, it took a crook.

Augment is up and down the other,
At least she knows all that!
But from the root or from the fifth,
And which was sharp or flat?

Oh fie, she cried in abject
frustration, I'll never find the song!
He's showing off his erudition
When I can't come along!

---

*Keith Snell and Julie MacIntosh Johnson
are publishers of some of the most highly
regarded series of basic music theory books.

When a Maestro Teaches The Piano

To teach me
You must descend
From a high mountain,
Remembering how it was,
Especially not forget when
Love of music was all you had,
With clumsy, flailing, boyish hands
That could not meet your lofty goals
Nor tell the story that you heard inside,
When hope was all that accompanied dreams
And moods turned dark when reaching up, you often
Fell.

A thousand free throws before one hits!
A million puzzles before one piece fits!

Oh, but glorious, sunny day–
I think I'll try again,
And someday soon, play!

Imposter?

Sometimes I wonder if I imagine loving music?
When all goes wrong and my memory fails
Upon trying to play a melody I know.
In those times, what is to show for hours spent in
Devotion lent to my endeavor?

What makes me persist, or better said,
What makes me want to get out of bed and go on
When my song so miserably fails?

And then I wonder if I'm an imposter,
Not something no one's thought before, I know.
Some of us go through it more than others.
Women, of course,
Are bothered more than men
When we cannot play a score we know so well.

It's hell on wheels when that happens.
I hate the idea of continuing on,
Why, I ask myself, suffer all this pain
And melt down more times than one?

So do I set it aside just for the while, come back
And spend more hours in coming up to snuff?
Or take it as a final call that, though giving all,
I've failed to make the grade,
Though no one's grading me?

I play because I love the music that I hear inside
That must come out! Some days it's stuck there like
When the tide deposits shells upon the shore
Or takes them back with mean attack
And leaves me wanting more.

No Performance, Please!

I don't want to perform,
I don't want to recite,
I'll resist such an idea
With all of my might.
I just want to play
With particular delight
The masters of love
And romantical plight.

So give me Chopin
Or Liszt with the hair,
The sweetest Robert Schumann,
I really don't care,
But feed me no Berg
Or Schoenberg, as it seems,
Those modernists will destroy
The fondest of dreams
To play as I will
The most lyrical of scores–
With all those I'll succumb
To the loudest of snores!

Frustration

My biggest struggle in playing piano
Is not errors with notes
Or rhythm or tempo,
Or meaning or nuance,
Rubato or touch,
Or structure or pause,
Or how loud or how much.

It all seems like fingers
That fill holes in the dike.
What rubs me the worst?
It's my musical vision
That fails. And that hurts,
When through theory or practice
I can't seem to bring
My playing to perfection
That pulls at heartstrings.

I try and I try,
Each approximation much closer
To the goal I envision.
But some days I cry
In protest so futile!
The result that I coax
Seems embarrassingly puerile.

My vision so lofty
It stretches for miles
And rises so high
Approaching the skies.
But weep then I must
Because I lose trust
That the day will arrive
When my spirit will thrive
And perfection burst forth
To prove soul is alive.

But perfect will never be reached;
Seems patience is the lesson
That my experience does teach.

Memorizing Music

There's something abiding deep within
Thatseeks to be understood.
It beckons me and wants me free
To make my melody heard.

Has nothing to do with pure technique
In playing my piano,
Yet has everything to do with that–
A teacher told me so!

Thenmy teacher followed up,
Advised that I'll play best
To learn to memorize and then will
come nuances and all the rest.

But is that true or misses the mark?
It doesn't create space
To express nuance or push rubato,
Thoughsome think that's the case.

What it does, of this I'm sure,
Is liberate my ear,
Give some space, open the door
To a melody so dear.

It's clear that memory's not prime
But listening to what's below,
Thenhear the call to set music free
In luscious ebb and flow.

I should not worry as it seems.
First, hear the tune inside
Then memorize the notes I see
Until securely they abide.

Photo top r. and bottom l., courtesy of Elyse. Photo bottom r. courtesy of Jeff. Photo top l. courtesy of Ron.

Fig. 6 *The Duchess*' Christening Party guests (clockwise from top l.) Elyse Shafarman and Ann; Jeff Harris and Joe Torres; Joe is ready to play Beethoven's "Pathétique" sonata; Raven Crone from Nevada, joined the party on Skype.

On The Duchess
♫♪♫

"My piano is a metaphor for desire, love of life,
and gratitude for the opportunity to express myself—
and what Liszt said!"

> — Ann Grogan,
>   poet and pianist

"My piano is for me what a ship is to a sailor;
more indeed: it is my very self, my mother tongue,
my life."

> — Liszt

Fig. 7   Clockwise from top l.: Using a template to test the fit of a 5'7.5"
piano in the perfect living room space; first moment viewing arrival
of *The Duchess*, April 28, 2022; skillfully navigating some treacherous
stairs to her new home; Joe and Ann beaming in celebration of the
new arrival, finally in her place!

 Breathe*

You gave me space to breathe,
Helped me achieve my goals,
Held my hand when nothing worked
To sooth my soul
When fatigue set in and offered me the sin
Of sitting down and giving up.

You saw my vision
As it was and came to be,
And spent hours of your time
Listening to the melodies
That I heard and did pursue
So awkwardly at times,
No rhythm, no rhyme,
Just lust to try and express
What I liked best.
You liked some, too!
Lehár the best, as the *Merry Widow*
Our hearts blessed.

Our long journey came to rest;
The piano goal now reached,
The Duchess sings, so fine she is!
The dream I had you knew I'd find,
And at each step of my way,
Reminded me.

No adventure complete,
No search replete with rewards
But that they dwell not in one, but two:
The true meaning of me and you!

---

*In gratitude and with love to Ron Choy,my life
partner, who supported me for all ten months of
the search for my grand piano, *The Duchess.*

Frivolous

I'm going to be "frivolous"*
And I'm going to fly,
I'm going to laugh loudly
And I'm going to cry!

I'll buy my piano
Despite all your worries;
At my age I don't
Need your favor to curry.

So join me or not
And celebrate freedom,
Cultivate *your* dreams:
It's beyond time to seize them!

———

*A few friends expressed reservations when
I first spoke of my adventure to find my first,
and last, small grand piano. I was heartened
when Raven Crone, one of my besties, was
supportive throughout my journey and in
June 2022 attended my piano's christening
party.

A Fine Piano

Though an easy sell I'm not,
For a piano to suit me,
He* led me to my piano
And the rest is history.

"Keep the faith" he often said
As online my hand he held
And comforted me with assurances
To quell the fear I felt.

"Trust yourself" he reminded me,
"And do not ever doubt."
"Listen to your heart" he said,
"And it will all work out."

So blindly then I went along
With a process, oh, so strange.
Some days I felt like a stranger in
A land a bit deranged.

'Twas always something did not fit:
A touch sadly so foreign,
Not quite right the cabinet,
Or tones were much too thin.

But I soldiered on until the day
The answer came at last,
A custom one, the best readymade
So clearly would surpass,

And now I wait though I barely can
Tolerate delay,
Until at last my dream comes true
And I sit down to play!

———
*Bruce Nalezny, pianist, composer, Director/
Founder of *The Piano Gallery* and piano broker who
located *The Duchess* (bruce@finepiano.com).

Where is My Piano?*

The Duchess, whom I mean,
She must be wandering
Alone and in despair
In Never Never Land,
A stranger in a wild
And strange piano land.

Where is my golden girl?
Her glory not unfurled–
Not yet, but you can bet
She'll shine so well
As time will justly tell,
My fears to be dispelled.

If piano magic works,
The hammers soon will sing
And dulcet tones will ring,
Her glory days restored
Then soon from purr to roar
She'll interpret my sweetest score.

---

*It was almost intolerable to wait six months for my piano to be rebuilt, even if that was the current norm.

On Waiting For My Piano

She's just an idea now,
A wisp of wood but mainly smoke.
It clearly did get in my eyes
And some days surely made me cry
In grave despair, frustration even,
Though promised he that it will be!

And one day soon, since time does fly,
She'll ready to come home with me.
But now she languishes, us both alone
And dreaming of the other,
Coming closer day by day,
Soon to move inside the dream,
Dissolving there, or so it seems.

Being Part Cause

Thinking more about the query,
How did I happen to choose at last–
After trying so hard to find and play
Some 40 pianos that crossed my path?
A class lady, the M Steinway
And from 1928 she came,
Then stood among the dust and grit
So patient in wait for me to tame,
Her rough coat really showed her age,
With waning sounds of failing hammers,
Not suitable for any concert stage.

The piano broker who found her first
Declared her foundationally fit,
And piqued my interest when he said
With brilliant ivories she was equipped.
So being of history so appreciative,
As well as of all things traditional
(You see, I lived a former life
In times likely Victorianical),
How could I resist once I played
Those keys so pristinely appointed,
Then selected the hammers most suited to
Her potential to play the tones I wanted?

So like a bolt it came to me,
'Twas a waste of time to try to find
A readymade piano that clearly was
Someone's dream, but just not mine.
I thought some more about how it was
That I came to choose rebuilding;
Something about the creative element
From other choices was missing.
And then one day I considered folk music,
Each with a basic plan and style,
But each singer embellishes all within
To create music that does beguile.
Likewise I'll embellish my lady fair,
An integral part of the team I chose
To adapt her basic plan and style
While I have the joy of being *part cause*.

Seeking (Part 1: Unrequited; Part 2: Requited)

PART 1: Major thrills with minor doubts,
My odyssey to find
The object of all dreams sonorous:
The grand piano in my mind.

A simple tune I so preferred
But complexity I found,
From Berg to Ligeti* I shrunk in horror.
The tune I sought was round,
So, too, the tone, sweet, warm, and fine—
A stylish lady true I sought
But at first just could not find.

None fit my lover's overture;
Chord after chord I tried my best
To call her to my side,
But followed discord, then more indeed,
So often that I cried
And took time outs. I cannot lie,
I almost left the fray.
The more I wanted, the less I found,
Much to my dismay.

Just fun and bliss I so desired!
A refection of my dreams,
But more so of my soul and heart—
Impossible it seemed!

PART 2: So then what happened, some may wonder,
On October 16, '21?
The goal was reached at struggle's end,
The battle completely won!

Piano found, secured, and paid,
The project well begun,
The Warrior Woman went to sleep,
Her adventure now well done!

---

*Alban Berg (1885-1935), Austrian composer, Second Viennese School, who combined Romantic lyricism with the 12-tone technique; Gyorgy Ligeti (1923-2006), Hungarian-Austrian composer of innovative, contemporary classical music.

A Hundred Deaths

I died a hundred deaths*
And aged a hundred more,
I've tried to entertain myself
With many a piano score.
I learned ten tunes and more,
Trying to be patient,
And all I got is "wait some more"–
That's how my story went
Six months, then more,
Three weeks beyond the time
'Twas said I'd have to wait
Before the prize I'd find.
So was I right, or was I wrong
To follow my intuition
And wait some more and trust a lot
For my dream to come to fruition?

———
*How I felt in the sixth month after
contracting for *The Duchess* to be rebuilt.

The Process

Part of the process of buying a piano
Is nothing short of torture,
Especially when you cannot find
A readymade to give you pleasure,
But decide to pursue a harrowing adventure
To find "The One" who portends
In playing, a bliss without end—
That special piano, a historical treasure
When rebuilt to tell her story,
Will reach the imagined former glory
That lives within your mind.

But in the end, what will I find?
A foolish choice, or wisdom certain
To confirm the choice I made,
The path I took, the trust bestowed
On those who assured me
And represented that satisfied I'd be?

I live in hope, is all that can be said
Until my project is safely put to bed.

A Long Journey in Under a Year

It was less than a year ago
That a bee came under my bonnet,
When I started my search for a piano
And the writing of poems and sonnets.

It was far, far before that time
When I opened my heart to music–
The thrill of discovering melodies
Beyond what you'll find in "Chop Stick."

From Schumann to Schubert and more,
On 40-some pianos I played,
Testing tones and the touch, along
With a few new friends I'd made.

It took me a while to hear,
As I listened to what I could,
Next study, then let the wave
Reach the shore as it eventually would.

I'd been on Jason's journey,
Managed San Juan Teotihuacán,
Won the Peloponnesian Wars,
And met women like Lysistrata.

My argonaut finally at rest,*
The battles all well won,
The piano of my dreams came home,
My task was then well done!

The Duchess was finally moved into her new home
on Thursday, April 28, 2022. And was I happy?
Read on if you have any doubts!

The Duchess in Her Home!
(April 28, 2022)

Will life be long enough for me to sing all praises
That her tone and touch do raise up
Inside of me?

The Duchess whom I mean,
At last! At home! Starry smile in my eyes
As with tender rapture I bless
The golden coat she donned for me,
The ivory keys that so please
And shine in the amber waning light,
Aglow with shimmering beams of love.

For me, there is no other
But *this* lover, *this* treasure, *this* reward
For long days of endless waiting.
Silent now I am, no word, just her sound
So round and full. She speaks! I listen well
To hear the message that she tells:

What bliss on me befell!

So Odd to Notice

Another discovery–
I sit to the left of the Steinway lyre graphic!
The same sits to the right of middle C
That one can find *near* but not the middle of all keys.
Amusing, I never noted it when consumed in misery
In my search for my prize, my heart's desire,
My piano so fine, it sets my heart on fire!

A surprise was the lyre, beyond what I felt
When practicing my piece,
The Mendelssohn score that enthralls,
Though sometimes I plow through notes that are wrong,
Less often now I've received my angel wings
With which to play keys that pluck my heartstrings.

I was about to soar after rising this morn,
Skipping music appreciation remote,
To rush to *The Duchess* and together sing
Our song. So odd to note when stroking the lyre,
Being careful to just brush with fingers pristine
To not tarnish the keys or her cabinet's sheen,
The lyre sits to the right of middle C where I sat,
Both player and piano pretty, and pretty determined at that,
But all in all I could not contain my elation
To find my senses opening up (were they on vacation?).

Of a sudden I could hear as I composed a new sound
For each side-by-side note, so different I found
In contour and nuance–next noted my best
Required me to touch her fine keys
With great love, I could see.

So tenderly I played, a thousand times at least,
"Contemplation," and tried my very best
To say what I felt, and the composer felt, too;
Thus passed the first day, as time really flew!

The Duchess: Midnight of Day Two

I played 'til midnight and I swear
I heard more than I imagined I heard before.
I asked her for a different tone, a lighter sigh,
A slighter touch which she gifted me,
As we sang a nuanced song
Much sweeter than before.

Could it be that what I wish is what she gives?
The want I want is what she needs?
Can it be true that we are the One
I felt was possible and for which I longed?
Holding on to that belief,
Did I and those who cared along my way,
Create this soft dove who came to stay?

Home Alone

Home alone...delicious day
As I play my treasure fair!
I'm listening to the miracles there
I never knew or felt before
As I played each score
From sweet to ribald,
On my other lady fair,
*Ms. Bellamy.** Beautiful she, too,
Just like my *Duchess*!**
The both of them are blessed
And give blessings in return.
Each different, as I learned,
Each valued as I reflect
And will learn more, I do suspect!

---

*My high school spinet.
**My grand piano.

The Duchess, Day Four

I can make her speak and sometimes shout,
I can bring the sweetness from inside out,
But still I'm awkward in knowing when
To touch her soft but not lose power within
The sound I make. Will she break?
She's so lovely there! I almost despair to think
That I might harm a hair upon her golden head!
I dread I might not live up to what she brings
To my life to make it richer
Than any chest full of things that glitter!

The Duchess, Forever!

I am a mom who's now done in
With a process, oh, so visceral!
From head to toes and inside out,
My experience seems surreal.
"What experience?" you ask in puzzlement.
"You refer to what on earth?"
Remember (or imagine) this, please,
How you felt in giving birth:
Fatigue from head to toe, it hits
And drops me in my tracks
With the deepest sleep I've ever had;
I wonder if I'll come back?
It strikes at noon or perhaps at three
And lasts a couple of hours.
I can't resist and can't control
Mr. Morpheus and his powers.
No sign of depression or buyer's remorse,
Of that I'm so very sure!
It's just I'm happy with my new arrival,
My "infant" with tone so pure.
I scarce can leave her side to eat,
I check on her each moment,
I caress her case, her beautiful face
And bless the gift the goddess sent!

Fig. 8   At the June 16, 2022 Christening Party for *The Duchess*,
Ann prepares to entertain very patient guests with her first
ever composition entitled *2'16.5"* while Ron gets ready to turn
the blank page (see poem on page 63).

On Life

"Whatever you think matters—doesn't."

> — Roger Rosenblatt,
> *Rules for Aging*;
> American memoirist,
> essayist, and novelist

"I find that the most people's stress in life is created by taking themselves too seriously."

> — Anonymous

Fig. 9   Ready to practice! The small sign to the left reads: "Every time I play, it is an approximation. Every approximation is complete in itself."

Much is Given

To us whom much is given
And who are mainly driven
To express our soul
And be so bold
To share our joy in living,
Then we must give and share in return
Without expecting much,
No endgaming, no goal in sight,
Just sit quietly in ebb and flow,
Let go and rest in pure delight.

A Little Afternoon Prose

A life without passion lived–
How sad! I'm glad I chose otherwise,
To feel deep and wide and then besides,
To dare to do just what I chose
And share just what I felt.

To do other would be a lie
And would belie what I really believe.
I seek not to deceive
But tell my truth, express desire,
Admire the best of those like me
Who reach within then share without,
In kindness repose, and like the rose,
Their fragrant soul do share.

Needs and Wants

Needs and wants are far apart,
The first of body, the second, heart.
Both important to be sure,
Just one, our ills it will not cure
But two along with values known
Then happy, fruitful seeds are sown.

Bliss

It's never easy, is it, life?
Full of bliss but also strife.
Bittersweet or sweetly bitter,
Woes along our way do litter,
But also flights of fancy light
Our way and thus our souls delight!
One day up and one day down,
Then a smile and next a frown.
But surely one thing stands alone
Our woes and sins to soon atone,
And help survive the daily fray
To live to love another day,
And that is hope, or another word,
Optimism. It's not absurd
As some might say, but think on this:
'Tis the only thing that leads to bliss!

Happy Birthday!

Wish me Happy Birthday,
Because today it is.
A happy day I like to think,
And focus on the positive.

Yet living closer day by day
To the century mark, oh, yes!
Nearer to the fall than spring,
So fast, I must confess!

And yet reborn with morning sun
And songs of winged friends,
Reminding me on every day
The gift each moment does portend.

At Rest

Always tinged with disappointment
But never lacks delight,
Or dreams or passion set afire,
The story of my life.

Struggles yes, and sadness, sure,
But beyond those I learned to cope
And pursued as closely as I could
The holding on to hope.

For hope provides grand possibilities,
It's more than just a base,
It augurs well for flight unbound
Above the human race.

In flying then, I found my home,
Let go of all the rest;
As clouds pass by and storms move on,
My soul remains at rest.

Note to Self

I live an excited life. They say
Good for youth, but not for old.
"Pollyanna One!" Joan* said to me,
"Perhaps," I said, "at least I'm bold!"
At least I love, I play, I feel
And hope and pray and sometimes fail.
As years go on, at least I have
Sterling stories to regale.
Adventures many, truth I sought,
And valued much, intelligence.
But came it from these: mind and soul
And body, together, all made sense.
So still excited as I go,
Eyes open but in wonderment,
Loving those who cross my path
With love. And so a life, well spent!

———
*Joan Nelson, MFCC, friend and former therapist.

I Mind!

The act of self-realization is radical.
So says Lauren Berlant in *The Times*.
(*New York Times*, that is; I forget when.)
But then, she's right!

It's not protest or socialism that gives fright
But going against the grain,
Not wheat, I mean,
But refer to the other,
When one does bother
"The regime,"
Upset the status quo as it seems,
Bash down the door
Or norms that do bore
The creative mind.

I mind, don't you?
You should.
I would if I could
Destroy all things
That conformity brings.

Such a great waste
To rush with great haste
To be the same!
Why not the reverse:
To stand out from the crowd
(Except that's not allowed
For "good" girls and boys)?
Speak out, act out, and just
Be yourself, without strife
Or anger or doubt.

Just go ahead and shout out
Who you are!
Love who you wish, marry or not,
Yawn at the common, rage at the stupid,
Speak up for justice!

I trust us to do right by all things,
Pets, environment, and the stars,
People, even more.
After all we are
All stewards of the world,
But more so, the self.

You are unique! Enjoy yourself!

Labels

The problem with labels is that
They give rise to judgments at best,
And inherently they include
Hierarchies of bad and good,
Things anathema to me you might know.
But if you don't, then I'll show
That those things I just won't brook,
Or stop to consider or look.
It's freedom I value the most,
Less to me, is nothing but toast.
For if I cannot live free
Then I surely cannot be me,
Nor can you, except in my mind
Where there you may find
The freedom to be fully you.
Don't be afraid, in truth,
To go there with boundaries set loose,
Brook anxiety and stress as they come
And prevail o'er distractions not fun.
The rewards I promise are many,
Your travails so puny, if any,
And soar as you will in delight,
To the heavens you'll surely take flight.

Seized

Sometimes I'm seized
And then so pleased
With a tune divine
Or even sublime,
Or a simple rhyme
That at the time
Tickles my fancy
And then I dancy
Around my kitchen
With the chicken
And the cow
Or maybe the sow.
We move so slow
But then must go
Faster yet until we get
Dizzy then, from the spin
Around the room,
Next with a broom
That we store there
And hold so tight,
A partner slim,
She's barely there.
We do not care
Because we delight
As moves take flight
And we take off,
Our hats do doff,
Our hair let down
And without one frown
We're free at last
To have a blast!

Response on Hearing From a Former Boyfriend

This chapter challenge is about the same
As it was so long before
When young, our paths did strangely cross,
A happenstance, of course.
The choice was ours: the "middle fork"
Or point of no return?
Each moment of our lives a choice,
With lessons to be learned.

And so we did, it occurs to me,
Flow down the river fast,
Make our choices, live in the beds
We made along our path.
But seems to me, if not to you,
The only purpose is
To experience life as it comes
Then in happiness repose.

Pull in our horns, stay closer home,
This moment prescient,
A gift to us to seize and then
Foretell our future's bent.
One thing I've learned from "Into the Wild,"*
I never thought before,
Happiness only comes at last
When shared, not waited for,
And shared in telling of our tales
That we struggled best we could,
Then found it deep within our souls,
As happy then we stood.

So who am I? What did I become?
Father? Mother? Sister, too?
Irrelevant. What I want to share
Is art, and to be understood.

---

*2007 movie; Sean Penn, Director/Co-Writer;
film adaptation of Jon Krakauer's book.

What I Know

There are things that one may wish for
And things that one may know,
Times when two are one
And times when we're alone,

Moments when we wonder if
We'll make it out alive
Or if the worth is really there
For times that we did strive?

And then again we know that ups
Can't be without those downs.
We can't fly high and touch the sky
Unless we stand our ground.

We can't feel calm and peace within
Unless we go without
And give to others needing us
And loving us, no doubt.

There's clarity if we sit still
In silence and just note
The blessings that we truly have
That keep us all afloat,

And reach inside to stem the tide
That threatens to disappear
The joy residing deep within
When happiness is shared!

So grateful then, I feel at last
To think of my true friends,
My life's adventures and good health, too,
And the moment that's at hand!

Challenges

What is it then, that challenges bring?
(The "why?" is totally irrelevant,
Unless, of course, religion prevails
With its many "shalls" and "shants.")

If our mission is to experience joy
And be kind to others, too,
Then we must seize upon the chance
To our best natures be true.

When our world becomes so starkly depressing,
It's still our choice after all,
To step into the light and live our values
And not on negatives to dwell.

Challenges test the depth of desire,
The breadth of knowledge we've learned.
Our spirits tell us how to obtain
The things for which we've yearned.

If outer worlds become unglued,
Take time to look inside
And hold those close who love us well,
Until peace within abides.

The Distaff Band

The man? Of few words, but the woman?
Loquacious like the distaff band
Who loves to flourish
And thoughts do nourish
And lives and thrives in ornamentation land.

Life...Again and Again!

I'm a fashionista first,
A pianist second, if at all.
That's my call to make, is it not?
Perhaps better said
(Before I trot off to bed)
Is that I first danced when I was young,
And with Crayolas found my calling
(It's sure not singing!),
Then moved on to work with pen,
Calligraphing my way through thick and thin
Until at last I found the muse
That took my hand and so did choose
To bring to life the sound within
And through music bring *me* to life again.

Right!

Aristotle had it right
About what prevents any plight:
A bit of pepper,
A pinch of salt
And it'll turn out all right.

But if you try to express
Any thought of pure excess,
You'll find out soon
That you'll surely rue
That day and all the rest.

To Pen a Score

To pen a score or sing a song,
To lift paint brush or dance along,
To make art gives all meaning
To what soul is...life's wounds forgiven.

Disturbing

It disturbs my friend, the political scene–
But the Ukraine* war makes me scream!
I wish it were clear just what to do,
To stop the mayhem that monster Putin does spew.

Then there's ethics to consider
In hosting Russian conductors.
Should we take umbrage with those musical leaders
Who welcome them as good neighbors?
Or should we cancel recitalists and then all the songs
Of those with Putin who do go along?

So what about Wagner, a friend of the Nazi?
Or men who thought women should never be free?
For that matter, it seems,
Do we remove from the US Capitol,
The portrait of George? Is that so rational?
And is it fair to wipe out history,
Because with "woke" eyes we now see
The blunder and sins of all intolerance,
No less than war waged without any sense?

I'm left in a quandary about those who stay silent,
Claiming they are "apolitical."
Is that consent
To what those in their name, do to the rest,
And think they stand higher than all of the best?

---

*Without provocation, Russia's leader, Vladimir Putin,
launched a large-scale, deadly invasion of and genocidal
war against Ukraine on February 24, 2022.

What is Creativity?

What is creativity?
The source of libido I say.
Freud got it wrong,
Reversed the order,
Created disorder
In our understanding
Of human beings.

The star?
The urge–not to merge,
But to self-express,
No matter what or how,
So long as true and truly said,
Thought out or not,
Considered well and deep
Or from our sleep
Retrieved as dreams
Or just a scream of bliss.

T'would be amiss, of course,
To leave out the brain,
A comely part of love's refrain,
A crucial part that leads to pleasure
When we treasure both the art and thought.

But take away the feeling
And you're left dealing with the mind alone.
Where to go with that
If feeling leaves us flat?
In prison as it seems, the ball in handball court,
In short, careening endlessly,
No tether to the soul,
No way to call her out in sigh or shout,
But shut within and suffering.

I'll take them both, the brain and heart,
But most of all, I'll opt for art!

Response.1:
With All Good Intentions*

Some things need not be said, but heard.
The World of Light transports as it transfixes
Those who see and hear, but do not speak.
There is no need for words when hearts connect
With others or with thought, as we cathect
What is, with meaning.
There is no darkness that exists
That beauty cannot o'er come
And it's easy to forget
That we are One.

Listen! Can't you hear
The melody of love
That resides in you, in me,
In living beings, and the soul of those
Who move beyond to greater things?

From deepest despair we lift each other up
To hear again what we know:
Let go, attend, listen to what's inside of you,
Then offer up your soul with all good intentions.
There's no monster lurking there in his lair
Whom we cannot defeat, dissolve, dismiss
By just allowing who we are to shine,
In trust that someone, somewhere will hear us cry,
Will hear us speak out from our deep and keen desire
To love.

---

*Inspired by the request of B.N. to write a poem about the effort
and good will underlying the creation of things of beauty as
opposed to the ease of their destruction and extreme fragility.

Response 2: Hope *

What I see in my mind
Comes out in words;
I listen to the pictures there,
And paint the sounds I hear
On my piano fair,
And dance the dream I'm dreaming there
In poems—nothing important
To anyone but me, because what I see
Is only there, inside my mind.

It all comes down to creativity.
Delay an instant and the thought abates,
Wait some more and it's gone
And my song is lost forever more!

I must move along my groove
When rhymes strike deep,
Perhaps in sleep, then I rise up,
Open my dream book,
Take up my pen and write.

What delight to seize the thought,
Pursue the dream,
Weave a carpet without seam
Into whole cloth of rainbow threads!

I live with hope the best will come of it
When facing down the darkest days.
It's in sharing that the sun's rays come
To warm our hearts, inspire the dream,
Help us capture thought in poem or note—
The music there as it always is,
Ours to seize, create, and give.

———
*Inspired by the request of B.N. to write a poem about the effort
and good will underlying the creation of things of beauty as
opposed to the ease of their destruction and extreme fragility.

Endless

"To leave something they can use,"
Says Alice Walker* from her muse,
Is what she wishes for her legacy
Of a life well lived and purely free
To express herself. I don't disagree.
On love, she goes on to digress
To say that in the heart it's blessed
And does grow. A kiss goes on
Forever more, a halcyon
Of bliss, and the possibility of love?
Endless.

Now "on her way out," she says with intent
(But this I wish she would not present).
Age 78, is that so late?
Depends if you've lived, or lived to wait.
She's lived to speak her honest truth,
And write it out and not be loath
To share with us her stories many.
And the life beyond she does foresee?
Endless.

---

*Interview April 13, 2022 on CBS-TV with Gayle King,
concerning Walker's book, *Gathering Blossoms Under
Fire*. Walker is an American novelist, short story writer,
poet, and social activist. In 1982, she became the first
African-American woman to win the Pulitzer Prize for
Fiction, which she was awarded for her novel *The Color
Purple*.

Sailing

Did you know, H.D. Thoreau,
How famous you'd become?
A million times beyond your dreams
And shine beyond the sun.

So brilliant, yes, in eons past,
Until you died at last.
"Now comes good sailing," as you said
In the moments before you passed.

1862 marks the year,
The date was on May 6th
When a troubled world said goodbye
And you departed quick.

Yet so true it is, you live today!
Your message still extant.
So apt for culture google-ites
Who often indulge in cant.

"Eschew it all in favor of
A life that's purely simple;
Look at the pond, which is your soul,
On nature do not trample."

"Look deeply in," you advised us all,
"Let 'busy' not you define,"
With only this, you'll be prepared
To happily sail on.